Dear Sherx

I hope you enjoy this book.

Sincerely,

Simon Okolo.

ROOTED IN LOVE

ESSAYS, STORIES, AND IMAGES OF

ONE VIBE AFRICA

SIMON JAVAN OKELO

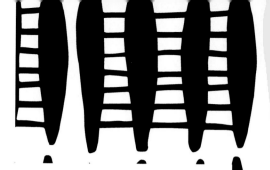

THE PHOTOGRAPHY

Rooted In Love contains amazing pictures from Kenya and Seattle. There are pictures that I took by myself. There are also pictures taken by photographers from Kenya like Otieno Okong'o of Krushal Entertainment. Currently based in Sweden, Otieno was one of the first photographers to capture One Vibe activities between 2008 to 2013 in Kenya.

In 2014 I went to Kenya with Corvus Eye Media and Tackett Films, which are thriving film and media production companies from Seattle that accompanied me to take photos and videos of our work in Kisumu. In 2015 we partnered with Meg Stacker, a New York-based photographer, who also traveled to Kenya with me to start Piga Picha Project, which is a photography training program that is focusing on giving children in the slum cameras and training them on photography skills as the children take pictures around the slum. Some of the photos in "Rooted In Love" are from Piga Picha Project, which is still ongoing in Kisumu, Kenya, through One Vibe Films.

I give compliments and credits to all the photographers who worked with me to document the Madaraka Festival in Seattle between 2014 to 2019. You can learn more about some of the photographers in the testimonial section, where some of these amazing, talented, and renowned photographers shared their stories. Some of the photos you will see in "Rooted In Love" are also from other One Vibe Africa events held in Seattle between 2014 to 2019. These include Kijiji Night at Seattle Art Museum, International African Stage at Upstream Music Festival & Summit in 2018, and at Seattle Theatre Group's Neptune Theatre in 2019. Please check out the acknowledgments section towards the end of the book. It contains more information about contributing photographers.

INTRODUCTION

In 1997, my mother and a group of women from our community started an orphanage home known as Young Generation Centre, which served hundreds of children in our community. It served as an orphanage until 2013 when I was given a chance to lead the transformation of this historic space into a Creative Hub operated by One Vibe Africa, which is a non-profit organization that I founded in 2008 in the wake of the post-election violence in Kenya. I serve as the Founding Executive Director of One Vibe Africa in Seattle, Washington, where I currently live and also in Kisumu, Kenya, where most of One Vibe Africa's activities are being implemented. I am confident that the approach that I used to grow One Vibe Africa from a reggae deejay crew to an internationally recognized organization can help donor-dependent projects in Africa and other parts of the world transform into creative hubs similar to Young Generation Centre where One Vibe Africa is based.

One Vibe Africa is the only organization started and managed by youth raised in the Manyatta slum in Kenya (including myself), which has programs in Seattle and collaborates with artists from Ghana, Nigeria, Uganda, Tanzania, and other parts of the world. It's extremely rare to find an organization or company started by young people from the slum and kept consistent and impactful for over ten years. One Vibe Africa is helping bridge the gap between rapidly developing tech industries in Seattle and Africa, and local artist communities. We believe the creative community has an important role to play in the global digital village being built by companies like Microsoft, Amazon, and Google in both parts of the world. I hope to use the success we have had in Kenya and Seattle as a blueprint that will be replicated to transform orphanage homes in Africa into

Creative Hubs. I grew up in Young Generation Centre, the orphanage home
started by my mother, and this allowed me to learn first-hand the challenges
people growing up in the slum face and how to solve them through locally
developed ideas. When I worked as the Field Director for Solace International
between 2005 to 2010 in Malawi, South Sudan, Liberia, Ghana, Uganda,
Tanzania, and Kenya, I also learned that many youths living in the slum in
those countries experience the same challenges I faced growing up in Manyatta.
After traveling and working in over six countries in Africa, I determined that
I could be useful to people in the slum in Kenya and those countries that had
slums. With a vision to transform places where people lack basic needs like
running water and reliable electricity to a life of dignity and an environment that
promotes self-esteem.

In December 2007, a day after I voted in the general election, I traveled to Ghana
and then to Liberia, where I was working on a project that was led by the elder
sister of the former President of Liberia, Madam Ellen Johnson Sirleaf. It sought
to turn a notorious prison into a vocational school. Working on this high-level
project provided the opportunity to work with the first female President in
Africa. In collaboration with the local government and the United Nations,
we were given a large helicopter to ship construction material to our project site
monthly.

Even though I was in Liberia, my mind was on the news about the events that
followed the election in Kenya. Contrary to the expectation of the majority of
the country, the results released, were not in favor of the opposition leader. In
the weeks that followed the elections, politicians mobilized communities along
ethnic lines, and violence began rocking the country from Nairobi to Kisumu.
Kisumu—an opposition stronghold—was extremely polarized. Unfortunately,

the violence spiraled out of control, and by the time the peace deal was signed on February 29th, 2008, thousands of people had died.

Prior to the end of the post-election violence, I traveled to Kenya to help relocate my mother and children living at the Young Generation Centre. Manyatta was dangerous with consistent police raids, women being raped, and chaos painted the whole town. There are people from the Kikuyu ethnic group that lived in Kisumu for as long as I could remember, but this post-election violence forced many of them to flee. Their properties were razed by fires and demolished to the ground by angry residents. In other parts of the country where the Kikuyu were not the majority, and they were suspected of having voted for the incumbent, they were also kicked out of town. For example, in Eldoret, a group of Kikuyus who had run away from their houses to seek refuge in a church were locked in the church and burnt to death. In the central parts of the country where the Kikuyu were the majority, members of the Luo community were also kicked out of their homes and killed like wild animals. This cycle of hatred and violence totally spiraled out of control, but I chose not to be involved in the violence or fuel it in any form. Instead, I worked to figure out how music could mobilize these warring factions to unite.

In April 2008, after the post-election violence subsided, I organized the first concert in Kisumu. Many people were still afraid to hold public gatherings, and people were still commonly seen carrying weapons. The success of this concert inspired me to turn my DJ company known at the time as One Vibe Entertainment into One Vibe Africa, a non-profit organization that now serves communities in Kisumu and Seattle. My crowning achievement is turning Young Generation Centre into a Creative Hub that has now served over 1,500 youth. Another crowning achievement is the move of the Madaraka Festival from Seattle to Kisumu. Since 2014, Madaraka Festival was held at The Museum of POP Culture in Seattle, WA. On August 3rd, 2019, I moved the festival to Kisumu, where it attracted over 4,500 attendees and established itself as the only festival dedicated to preserving the music and culture of people around Lake Victoria while attracting the diaspora to visit Kisumu where Obama and Lupita Nyong'o hail from.

One Vibe Africa is a unique organization that has turned into a movement beyond what I imagined. At the time, I wanted to create an alternative to the violence that had rocked my community. I thought that giving youth music instruments instead of guns would be the alternative. Now One Vibe Africa is an organization that provides people with joy, inspiration, empowerment, and jobs instead of desolation. When I was growing up in the Young Generation Centre from 1997 to 2010, we were over sixty children and youth crammed in a small compound that was not designed to accommodate more than twenty people. During the week, we had a primary school that served over one hundred students daily. Basic needs, like food and clothes, were scarce, and we had to depend on donors and well-wishers to survive. This life of dependency was the opposite of what my mother was known for prior to the opening of the Young Generation Centre.

My mother was the first woman to purchase a second hand Nissan Sunny Saloon car, which was not an easy thing for a woman from our community to do at the time. She was also the first person to install electricity, which opened up our community for business, and even tenants who would not otherwise move to our neighborhood moved into our compound before it was an orphanage home. My mother was an entrepreneur who used money from her businesses to help children who had been rendered orphans as a result of the HIV epidemic that was rampant in Kisumu in the 1990s.

Since 2013 One Vibe Africa runs an Education, Music & Art Program (EMAP) that has kept over 1,500 youth engaged in Visual Art, Traditional African Music, Dance, Guitar & Vocals, Poetry, Theatre, Fashion, Photography, and Filmmaking. These positive activities take place at the Young Generation Center (YGC) in the heart of the sprawling Manyatta slum in Kisumu, Kenya.

The objectives of the Education, Music & Art Program are to provide quality education to students through sponsorship opportunities, act as a safe space for youth to share experiences, stories and projects, and give youth a platform to express themselves through music and art, while also helping preserve culture by teaching youth traditional music, storytelling, film, and photography. One Vibe Africa's Education, Music & Art Program is partly funded by proceeds from social businesses that I developed that include One Vibe Films, which produces content for clients while training budding filmmakers. If you go to YouTube, you will find a video series called Made In Kisumu, which is one of the projects of One Vibe Films. We were also responsible for creating a short film about the premiere of the Black Panther movie, which happened in Kisumu before the global premiere. The star, Lupita Nyongo, is from Kisumu. Lupita sponsored over one thousand high school girls to attend the screening of the movie, and One Vibe Africa was given the opportunity to film and document the whole experience.

One Vibe Studio, which records music & preserves culture by recording traditional music, is another social business based at the Young Generation Centre. My team and I are currently working with Omena Band, which consists of elders from Mbita, Kenya. We work with these established artists in our rehearsal space — most bands in Kisumu practice there on a day to day basis. Parents also sign up their children for our music, and dance classes, and some parents also take adult classes that include learning how to sing and play musical instruments.

Madaraka Festival has been one of the most consistent African events celebrating the Diaspora. The festival has been dubbed: "a night to remember" by Northwest Music Scene, "a premier African-influenced festival" by YES Magazine, and a "globally oriented event" by Humanosphere Magazine. Madaraka Festival brings Africa's finest musicians and creatives together with world-renowned artists and innovators for a celebration of music and civic purpose. In 2019, this international cultural extravaganza was the culmination of an entire week of activities happening in Africa for the first time, and it featured live music, storytelling, poetry, exhibitions, workshops, and a film festival. Proceeds from Madaraka Festival go towards One Vibe Africa's Education Music and Art Program.

Since 2014, proceeds from Madaraka Festival have helped One Vibe Africa build One Vibe Studio, One Vibe Films, and produce Madaraka The Documentary, which is an original work that embodies the spirit of liberation while fostering partnership and collaboration among filmmakers, innovators, and entrepreneurs across Africa and the Diaspora. Madaraka Festival has also helped One Vibe Africa galvanize over 15,000 Africans in the diaspora through a consistent Pan-African annual event and engage over thirteen million people through digital impressions.

Madaraka Festival's relocation to Kisumu from Seattle allows One Vibe Africa to promote Africa as an ideal international trade and tourist destination for lovers of music, arts, culture, and technology. We'll use the momentum from Madaraka Festival in Seattle to create a bridge between Seattle and Kisumu through the people drawn to the event and One Vibe's impactful work across the world. We have positioned Kisumu as the first African city to host the Madaraka Festival. We hope to expand the Madaraka Festival to other countries where One Vibe intends to expand its presence. Historically events like Madaraka Festival are far-fetched for Kisumu and cities along Lake Victoria, which is a region with immense potential but needs visibility provided by events such as Madaraka Festival. We believe the Madaraka Festival is poised to help bolster tourism and travel in this region before expanding to other parts of Africa.

One Vibe Africa is now known as the hub of the African diaspora because of the consistent events we organized in Seattle since 2012. In 2016 we started the One Vibe African Dinner experiences at Café Avole on Rainier Avenue. Each of these dinners features an authentic meal made by a Seattle based chef from a different African country every time we host these intimate dinners. Out of the 55 countries in Africa, we've had over 30 chefs from over 30 countries in Africa that have served dinner at the One Vibe African Dinner Experiences.

Over the 30 dinners, we've had more than 600 attendees from all over the world. Our attendees include people from all backgrounds who love good food and learning about African culture. These dinners have shown us the diversity and support of the Seattle community. We've experienced so much laughter and joy as we celebrate the different cultures while building community. One couple that met at one of these dinners in October 2018 got engaged at Seattle Art Museum during One Vibe Africa's Kijiji Night in February 2019. A few months later, in August 2019, I was privileged to officiate their wedding. What I love about One Vibe African Dinner Experiences, is we are truly creating a family.

Diaspora Connect is a video podcast that One Vibe Africa also produces in Seattle to help demystify diaspora life. If you go to One Vibe TV, our YouTube Channel, you will be able to watch episodes of Diaspora Connect that features international and local artists and leaders in Seattle. Diaspora Connect allows Africans and African Americans to learn about their shared heritage through stories and also allows other viewers to learn about Africa from Africans instead of the mainstream media that peddles an image of Africa that is not accurate.

One Vibe Africa also partners with Seattle Art Museum to present the annual Kijiji Night at Seattle Art Museum since 2015. Kijiji means village in Swahili. Kijiji Night has attracted over 3,000 attendees since its inception. Kijiji Night brings the spirit of an African village to the Seattle Art Museum during Black History Month through live music, storytelling, poetry, and fresh African food provided by local Seattle based African chefs. Kijiji Night also features a reading of excerpts from books authored by African and African-Americans.

Kijiji Night helps decrease neighborhood tension and community deterioration by uniting the collective African community for Black History Month. In the '60s and '70s, Seattle's Central District neighborhood was more than 70% black. However, as Tyrone Beason of the Seattle Times wrote in 2016, "Today, less than one-fifth of the population is black, with whites moving in such huge numbers in the space of a couple of decades, they've become the majority for the first time since the Eisenhower Administration, when there was a sizable Jewish presence in the area."

The Central District is not the only Seattle neighborhood to be gentrified or to experience increased neighborhood tensions as racial lines are drawn over real estate. Seattle is experiencing a boom of development as waves of tech workers with high salaries move in, pushing long-time residents and communities of color out. Tensions are on the rise, and getting people to listen to each other is increasingly difficult. Kijiji Night seeks to bring people together, center the

African experience, and use art to tap into people's innate sense of empathy and humanity. As people are pushed farther afield, it can be harder for them to organize or have central spaces where they can build community. As Seattle's African and African American communities continue to be displaced and pushed farther out of the city, it is vital that they still have spaces that are their own. Through our podcast "Diaspora Connect," African Dinner Experiences, and ongoing programs, One Vibe Africa is creating a consistent and agile space for this community to be represented in Seattle.

Young black men and women in America are in danger. Not only must they go through the typical struggles of adolescence and deciding what they want to do with their lives, but they must also struggle to overcome systemic barriers to their success. One Vibe counteracts this by offering professional networking opportunities to young people within our community. Sometimes this looks like personal one-on-one meetings, and sometimes One Vibe is able to connect youth to an internship or professional experience. By centering One Vibe as a movement led by youth mentored by me directly, One Vibe Africa is helping African youth tap into the creative part of their brain to think imaginatively about how they might design their future.

I wrote "Rooted in Love" as part of an inspiration that came to me when I was reviewing an exercise I was asked to do by Dee Endelman and Steve Benson. They were my colleagues at Generating Transformative Change, which is a unique leadership development program I attended in 2011 and 2012 right after I moved to Seattle from Kenya. At that time, I was not sure how to articulate my vision for One Vibe Africa, but what Dee and Steve knew was that I was a great storyteller. Due to my storytelling abilities, they asked me to imagine what One Vibe Africa would look like in the year 2024. They asked me to write a fictional story about a girl who benefitted from One Vibe's work.

Dee and Steve's request resulted in the story of Farida. Although a fictional story, it serves as a vision concerning the growth of One Vibe Africa. Since I wrote this story for them in 2012, I regularly review it and am pleasantly surprised that the things I wrote in the story are manifested. While you read "Rooted In Love," you will learn that although some of the places described in the life of Farida are fictional, they depict the real-life story of the majority of the youths that benefit from One Vibe Africa. I also deliberately picked a female character to honor my mother, my sisters, my wife, my daughters, and women who have been extremely influential in my personal growth and development of One Vibe Africa.

Simon Javan Okelo
Founder and Executive Director
One Vibe Africa

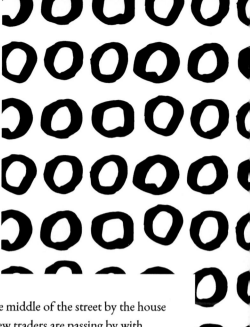

It's February 20, 2024, and I'm standing in the middle of the street by the house where I grew up in Kibra slums, Nairobi. A few traders are passing by with heavy loads on their bicycles, heading to their shops along the roadside. The street gets busier as the day gets brighter. The trader's bicycles are a work of art and innovation. Fabricated with extensions and at least four extra handlebars to provide room for hanging items for sale – they are supermarkets on two wheels. All items are sold in small quantities and packaged in clear plastic containers for display. The shopkeepers unpack all their goods in the morning and pack them up every evening for storage.

I grab my jacket and try to cover myself to keep warm. The zipper is broken, making it hard to protect myself from the cold that is making me shiver. As the street begins to fill with merchants and shoppers, I turn to the familiar act of packing and unpacking my father's bicycle shop.

Nairobi is home to millions of people from all corners of the globe. Many residents of the city under the sun live in the green leafy suburbs that I have heard of in the news through my dad's transistor radio. The eastern part of the city is primarily made up of three- to six-story flats built to accommodate working-class families. While the population of the entire city seems to grow by the minute, the majority of the population continues to live in various slums that surround Nairobi. The slums border affluent neighborhoods, drawing many people to live there. They work in the bungalows and big homes for meager earnings as housemaids, cleaners, and performers of household chores that the homeowners aren't willing to do themselves.

In contrast to the other merchants, my dad's bicycle shop only sold musical supplies and instruments. He could play more musical instruments than I could count. My dad would spend his days repairing and tuning instruments, replacing parts, modifying parts for those he couldn't replace, and purchasing broken instruments that were unfixable to be used to fix others in the future. My father was a legend from the vast streets of the city to the narrow paths of the slum. Every musician and music enthusiast either told a story about him or referred someone to him. I, therefore, grew up with strangers calling me by my father's name—in very unlikely places around the city.

I built a lot of muscles from helping my father push his bicycle music store to the street and back home each morning and evening. Because of my build, many people had a hard time discerning whether I was a boy or girl. I played soccer better than most boys, I was a key sprinter on my school's athletic team, and I was informally known for my musical talent. When I was eight years old, a tourist came to our shop with a broken guitar - a thief had tried to steal it, and while the man was able to get away, the guitar broke in half. A local hostel referred him to my dad, who was able to repair it. When the man came to pick up the guitar, he found me playing it. The tourist took a video of me and posted it on YouTube, where the video went viral.

My mother's whereabouts have always been a mystery, as my father never discussed her much with me. Rumor had it that she was a foreign musician who was born to a white missionary family. As a young adult, she came to Nairobi to learn about her parents' missionary work. She loved the city, and during her time here started a band in which she was the lead singer. My dad was hired to repair band members' musical instruments and work as a sound engineer. The band quickly gained popularity beyond Nairobi, touring many parts of Africa and Europe. One day, my dad returned to Kibra. I was less than a year old. No one saw my mom again. My dad never talked about his adventures around the world, or why he returned to the slums after living a glamorous tour life. He simply said this was home. While this was his home, I didn't feel like it was mine. I wanted to experience the world outside of Kibra slums.

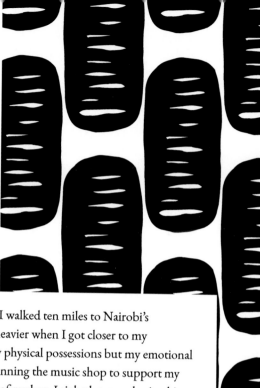

Finally, the day came for me to leave. As I walked ten miles to Nairobi's Machakos Bus Station, my bag became heavier when I got closer to my destination. The bag carried not only my physical possessions but my emotional ones too. Dropping out of school and running the music shop to support my father weighed heavy through the straps of my bag. I sighed, remembering his frail stature during his last year of life. I would set up the shop and then return to our home and bicycle him to the store for the day. During moments like this, I thanked my father and his shop for helping me build my strength to manage such a heavy load. Now, as I climbed onto the Kisumu-bound bus, I felt my body slowly sinking into the grey synthetic-leather seat. I tried to avoid hearing the grumbling from my stomach. It's amazing how my stomach rebelled after missing meals for three straight days. Not knowing what might happen day-to-day, I decided to save every penny from the sale of my father's music shop.

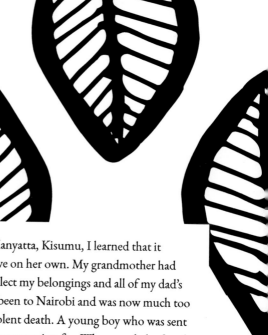

During my father's burial ceremony in Manyatta, Kisumu, I learned that it was taboo for a young girl of my age to live on her own. My grandmother had suggested that I go back to Nairobi to collect my belongings and all of my dad's items that I could salvage. She had never been to Nairobi and was now much too scared to visit after my dad's tragic and violent death. A young boy who was sent by a gang leader visited my dad to collect a protection fee. When my dad refused, I witnessed as the boy shot my ailing father several times.

As my father's body fell to the ground, his blood splattered on my legs and the shop. The boy turned the gun towards me. I ran to the back of the shop to shout for help he shot at me, I heard a click—he was out of ammunition. A mob quickly surrounded the shop. They descended on the killer and lynched him before my own eyes. In the process, we lost most of my father's tools because the mob used them as weapons. They threw whatever they could find on the thief, rocks, musical instruments, anything they could get their hands on. Then they lit a fire that consumed the little boy before the police arrived to collect his lifeless body. I sold what was leftover in the city and planned my departure.

I slept through most of the scenic bus ride across the Rift Valley towards Lake Victoria in the west. The bus arrived in Kisumu late in the evening. As we arrived, I spotted my grandmother through the window, accompanied by Sharon. I had first met Sharon at my dad's funeral, where she had sung a hymn for the gathering. After her song, I overheard people talking about One Vibe's Creative Hub that Sharon frequented. I could not hold back the tears streaming down my cheeks as I felt the warmth of my grandmother's body tightly holding mine. I finally opened my eyes after the long embrace to find Sharon also holding onto my grandmother and me. I had never before been openly emotional. My father taught me to be tough, even in the midst of the greatest adversity.

We arrived home after a long, exhilarating, and terrifying ride on the bicycle taxis from the bus station. The bicycle taxis are popularly known as "boda bodas" in Kisumu. They weave fast through the dark streets, between cars, pedestrians, and motorbikes as they move towards their destination. Sharon and I shared the same seat on one bicycle while my grandmother rode on another, with my bag between her and the cyclist. I found it odd to think that everything I owned was now in one bag wedged between my only known closest family member.

I am not sure when I went to bed that night, but morning came so quickly. If it were not for the sound of Sharon's voice singing while dressing to start her day, I would have slept longer. Sharon's voice was fading as she half-sung and half-talked to me about the plan for the day, which was primarily to visit One Vibe Africa's Creative Hub in Manyatta, Sijeh in Kisumu. I picked myself up, got out of bed, and dressed up to keep up with Sharon.

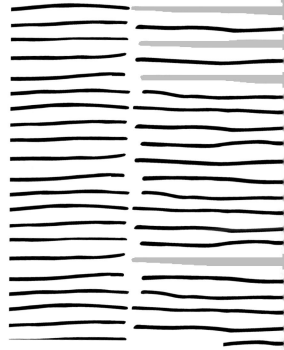

We had a quick breakfast with my grandmother, who was beautifully dressed in African regalia and ready for the world. We arrived at One Vibe's Creative Hub after a short ten-minute walk through the sprawling Manyatta slum. To my surprise, the moment we were all signed in at the gate, Sharon and my grandmother walked away, leaving me with Brian, who is the producer at One Vibe Studio. Brian was excited to show me around. I remember hearing him say that Sharon was involved with One Vibe as the instructor for voice and dance lessons.

Brian and I walked around One Vibe's Creative Hub, stopping next to the eucalyptus tree in the center of the complex. We stood in silence, staring at the mahogany and jacaranda trees surrounding the main building. The dry, hairy black pods carrying seeds of the jacaranda tree were dangling loosely from the trees lining the walls of the compound. Full of charisma from his voice to the way he moved, Brian asked that we turn around to face the main building and announced that he would start his tour of the entire facility from there.

The main building was a solid stone-built structure that looked like the image of a rectangular school building. It was colorful with the walls draped with paintings of various revolutionary African leaders, including Thomas Sankara, Winnie Mandela, and Wangari Maathai. We walked for about two minutes and arrived at the restaurant. Inside the high-ceilinged room painted bright grey and firebrick-red were about eight tables, each surrounded by eight chairs. Across the room was a bamboo counter surrounded by high bamboo stools. A "Fresh Fruit Bar" sign was hanging over the countertop. "This is where we serve fresh food, juice, salads, and smoothies to the community, and that is the wall of fame," Brian said as he turned around towards the other side of the room. "Celebrities who have eaten here put their signatures on that wall," he continued.

"Many people love it here. They call it 'Mama's Kitchen.' All the produce used in this restaurant is from our integrated Miti Ni Dawa farm. If you would like, we can visit the farm towards the end of the week," Brian said as we walked out to the next room. He then pointed at a sizable dark-brown mahogany door. Brian pushed the door open and let me in first. Brian quickly told me about his work and added that the studio had recently started making profits after its five years of operation. The studio was now consistently booked, sometimes making him work on projects overnight. As we left One Vibe Studio, we crossed paths with two artists who had rushed to catch Brian, before he left, to arrange a recording session.

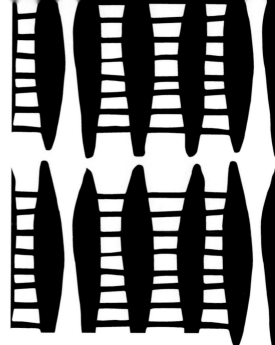

We arrived at One Vibe Radio, which was a room next to One Vibe Studio, but the door was locked as the presenters were on-air broadcasting the news. Only staff members were allowed in the room during a live news broadcast. Brian promised to bring me back there in due time. We then visited One Vibe Films, which was on the same floor as One Vibe Studio and One Vibe Radio. There were two young men and one girl glued to their computers. Two of them seemed to be watching videos and taking notes, and the other one was cleaning a camera. Brian introduced me briefly, and we continued with our tour of One Vibe Africa's Creative Hub in Kisumu, Kenya.

We went down the stairs to the first floor of the main building, where we started hearing music sipping through the cracks around the door and windows.

The first door was labeled "Rehearsal In Progress." Brian pushed it open and introduced me to Omena Band, who were practicing. We walked to the next room, which was also a rehearsal room, and saw Sharon leading a vocal class and waved at her as we walked to the next room, which was One Vibe Fashion. This is where all One Vibe merchandise was designed, produced, and distributed globally. The door was locked, so we peeped through the window and saw tailoring machines and computers. There were also personal effects on the tables in the room, so Brian announced that they might be out for lunch or an exhibition.

The stairs were fewer as we went down to the ground floor, where we had to check in again to access the One Vibe Tech Hub. "They are preparing for "The Kisumu Hackathon," Brian said as he pointed at a group of young women. "We provide the space for youth who may have dropped out of school for various reasons. They study tech here, and we connect them with tech companies in Seattle, where One Vibe Africa also has a presence. We have female tutors and volunteers from tech companies locally and abroad who support this amazing group. It's affordable to become a member, and we have more than three hundred members at the One Vibe Tech Hub."

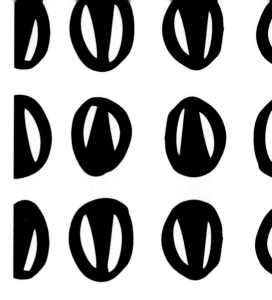

"I love it here, myself," Brian said as he pulled up a chair so I could sit while he guided me through the photos of One Vibe Dancers displayed outside the dance studio. We were both getting tired after touring the One Vibe Creative Hub. I was not sure how much more I was yet to see because I was already content with the much I had learned for the day, but then we began moving again this time away from the main building to the auditorium, the doors decorated with beautiful artwork. The event calendar on the notice boards on both sides of the entry area had long lists of upcoming events. From community gatherings, concerts, live radio events, conferences, to inter-school debates, the calendar was packed. Even though Brian was very young, he exuded the confidence of a champion. As he wrapped the doorknob with both of his tiny hands, I moved closer to give him a helping hand.

The oval auditorium was larger by the entryway and became smaller as it sloped downward toward the stage, with three walkways that split the rows of seats. The stained-glass windows rose towards the ceiling and were draped with thick black curtains that trailed the floor, while light playfully pierced the dark and empty hall. As we walked to each corner of the auditorium in silence, I marveled at the grand space for all that it was. Throughout the entire time, I kept thinking of all the people that have attended shows in the space as well as the performers. I could not help but picture myself on stage and connected with the audience like I was feeling connected to the empty space.

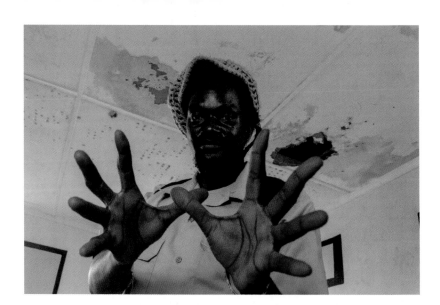

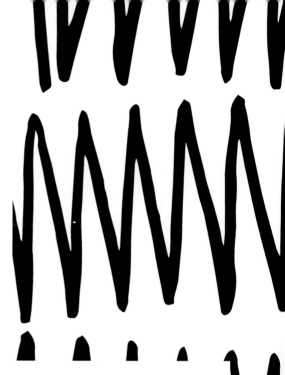

We moved on to the Arts Room located outside the auditorium. Several students and instructors were cleaning and setting up paintings and sculptures, while a few others were bent over worktops painting. The room looked like an art exhibition area. No one spoke a word, and everyone seemed to be so focused. Brian, also, was silent. I think he sensed the mood in the room and allowed me to learn by seeing and feeling.

A group of tourists met us as they came into the Arts Room, and we walked towards the Innovation Workshop that also served as the repair room for all sorts of equipment. The hissing sound of a soldering bit welcomed us into the room. There was an amplifier dismantled and placed on a worktop in one corner of the room. On the other side of the wall, hung guitars and trumpets that could have been undergoing refurbishments. Seeing these instruments in need of repair took me back to my father's bicycle shop and marked the beginning of my time as a beneficiary of One Vibe's work in Kenya. I started by helping in the Innovation Workshop, but now I run the Innovation Workshop in under two years of arriving in Kisumu from Kibra.

NJUGUNA WAGISHURU

SEATTLE RAPPER (THE PHYSICS). BANKING INDUSTRY

I first met Simon in 2011 at one of One Vibe's first fundraising concert at Nectar Lounge in Seattle through a mutual friend, Kamah of Kalamashaka. Simon quickly informed me about his background and the mission and history of One Vibe. His compelling story resonated with me.

In 2012, at the Legendary Lucid Lounge, Simon, Owuor Arunga, and I sat around a table. We created the concept and vision for Madaraka Festival, a major annual fundraising concert and cultural extravaganza for One Vibe in Seattle. We didn't know it then, but One Vibe would later gather an amazing group of local and international artists, leaders, and activists to make that vision a reality and take the organization to the next level of impact. That year we organized a successful Music to Empower Youth crowdfunding campaign and a sold-out Madaraka Festival, which I was proud to host, raising over $40,000 for One Vibe! Since then, we have built a fantastic local community dedicated to using the arts to impact the lives of youth in Kenya and Seattle positively.

As a Kenyan-American, I feel I have a duty to use the resources and opportunities I've been afforded to help my people, especially the youth back home, reach their full potential. One Vibe has empowered me to do this for young people in Manyatta, Kisumu, and I am infinitely grateful for the opportunity. One Vibe is using the arts to create new pathways to success and self-realization for Kenyan youth in a way no other organization is. More young people's lives are being lifted up each year by One Vibe. I am confident these young people will lead the organization, Kenya, and the continent to new heights.

RAYNA MILLER

COLORADO-BASED PHOTOGRAPHER

I first became connected to One Vibe Africa at the age of thirteen, when I traveled to the Manyatta slum in Kenya with my family. While I stayed and worked in the Young Generation Centre over the course of a month alongside One Vibe's Founder, Simon Okelo, I found my connection and network had grown to include people and places I had never imagined. My experiences with One Vibe Africa, within and outside of Africa, have been defining moments in my own life, much like the many children and young adults currently part of the Education Music and Art Program.

The attainability of a dream is often built upon the collective and its values. By creating a collective where the arts are seen as a powerful tool for individual and social change, One Vibe Africa makes dreams possible every day for the next generation. As an artist myself, I was able to find my own creative identity through One Vibe Africa's large network of artists and musicians.

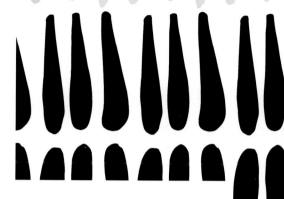

ROCKY DAWUNI
GRAMMY NOMINATED GHANAIAN ARTIST

I've had the great fortune of visiting, performing, and working on social initiatives in Kenya over the last few years. I became aware of Simon Okelo and the work that One Vibe was doing with the youth in Kisumu during one of my travels. As an African musician who has been dedicated to the importance of art and music in social development, I was extremely inspired by this effort and understood the long-lasting impact of this vital work in empowering the local community.

Simon and I became friends, and I observed One Vibe grow and expand its work over the years. Many friends of mine within the artistic community, and I have extended our support for One Vibe to enable it to grow its youth programs. I had the great privilege of performing at the Madaraka Festival in 2017, and I was struck by the amazing energy and excellent performances that all of the participating musicians brought to celebrate this great initiative.

YADESA BOJIA

SINGER, ACTIVIST, AND DESIGNER OF AFRICAN UNION FLAG

I first came in contact with Madaraka Festival by invitation of my friend, Simon Okelo. I attended the first Madaraka Festival, and the love, commitment, and dedication of those who volunteered made me look into it further. What I came to learn about the work that is being done through One Vibe Africa made me a lifetime supporter.

As an Ethiopian American, I know what life is like in the slums of African towns. I also know the unseen, undiscovered talents of Africa that life passes by simply because they don't have a place to nurture their talent or an organization that cares for their future. One Vibe Africa, with the help of the Madaraka Festival, is truly one of the organizations that do what is necessary. I proudly curated an art show for Madaraka Festival in 2015 that was made by kids from One Vibe's Education Music & Art Program in Kisumu. The talent that is being nurtured by this organization will surely benefit Kenya and, by extension, humankind. I was advised by my late mother to leave what I found better or the same as I found it, and Madaraka and One Vibe Africa are doing just that.

ANYIKO OWOKO

RENOWNED JOURNALIST, BLOGGER & SUPER PUBLICIST

I had known One Vibe Africa and their work for several years, beginning probably about five years back, when I used to work full time with Sauti Sol. I facilitated Sauti Sol's Soma Soma Initiative partnership with One Vibe. Through the emails and communication, I could tell that One Vibe's Team were good people with their intentions in the right places.

When we finally got to work together in 2017 during the launch of Madaraka The Documentary at Michael Joseph Center in Nairobi, it was wonderful to work closely with the whole team and to see their passion for education and vocational training. Going to Kisumu to see what they have been building over the years was so humbling. Something that got me asking myself, "What am I doing for my society?" I applaud One Vibe Africa for its contribution towards educating and enriching the lives of youth from Kenya and beyond. Through One Vibe, many young folks will know that art can save your life and can be a career. Thanks for having me work with you. I look forward to more.

WAEL "L" ABOU-ZAKI

CREATIVE DIRECTOR AT ZAKI ROSE

Culture is an embodiment of the person you are. My relationship with One Vibe began with a cultural understanding and a love for family. The story of Simon and the development of One Vibe inspired me to collaborate with the organization on the premise of telling the story by way of a documentary. Months later, with no hesitation, we traveled together to Kenya.

Memories are what we keep with us and the trips to Kenya; the family dinners, festivals, meetings, lifetime relationships, and global connections are driven by the passion for doing good for humanity. No prejudice, no walls, or limitations keep us from reaching our dreams. Although success is what we strive for, the journey is what I appreciate the most. The journey we've taken together has changed my life and will continue to do so. Peace & Love.

KELLY POWERS

SEATTLE BASED ONE VIBE VOLUNTEER

In our daily lives, we are bombarded with negativity and problems, making many of us feel helpless and grasping for ways to make a difference. Fred Rogers reminds us to "always look for the helpers; there's always someone who is trying to help." One Vibe Africa is composed of helpers, people who are dedicated to making a tangible difference, people who talk less and do more. I fell in love with the organization because the model isn't based on what Africans don't have. Instead, the focus is on what Africans do have; talent, curiosity, intelligence, resources, and drive.

As you look through this book, you will see photos that have captured some of the remarkable and joy-filled moments of One Vibe. You also will have the opportunity to peer into the future of this organization through the eyes of Farida and recognize what can happen when a person is able to follow his or her passions in a supportive and safe environment.

YIRIM SECK
SEATTLE BASED SENEGALESE-AMERICAN RAPPER & ACTIVIST

"A friend of mine invited me to a Cocktail Party, and it was there that I was introduced to Simon Okelo. As we got deeper into the conversation, I immediately knew I wanted to be involved with One Vibe Africa. Since my involvement, I've had the opportunity to perform at the 1st and 3rd annual Madaraka Festival in Seattle, sharing the stage with some of the most influential local and international acts such as Macklemore, Blitz The Ambassador, and Kenya's own Sauti Sol.

As a One Vibe Ambassador, I've helped with their annual fundraiser in raising money that directly supports One Vibe's Education Music and Art Program. I am continually inspired by One Vibe, and I will continue endorsing Madaraka Festival, as it has helped me find my purpose and the role I play in support of Africa and its people. One Vibe has now become a part of me."

DANA ROTH

FEDERAL REFUGEE OFFICER, AND PHOTOGRAPHER

If you are reading Rooted In Love, you are among friends. This is the story of a village empowering a village, and you, having picked up the book, have become a local. You have become an advocate. You have become an inspiration, whether you know it or not. As we follow Farida on her path to self-realization and inner strength, we see ourselves through her struggle. The same voids that she yearns to fill in her life have been healed, at one time in our lives, through the power of culture, arts, music, or technology. Once discovering this power, the desire is to share that potential... but how?

The catalyst behind this exponential inspiration is Simon Okelo, the founder and visionary behind One Vibe Africa. His infectious energy courses through the veins of every person he contacts. The work that One Vibe Africa does to empower youth in Kenya helps more than those in Kenya; it has inspired countless people all over the world. Rooted In Love tells the story of just a few who have discovered or used their strengths to help others. This book will inspire you to look deep inside yourself to find your niche in the puzzle of creating a more sustainable future. Welcome to the village of tomorrow.

TRUONG NGUYEN
PNW BASED / MULTI MEDIA CURATOR

My connection with One Vibe Africa started in 2016. I met Simon at Cafe Avole on Rainer Avenue in Seattle. I loved the fact that Simon was based in Seattle, but was making direct changes in Kenya and building a bridge to directly connect people in Seattle with Africa through collaboration on creative projects.

I'm a photojournalist and have been very involved in my Vietnamese community. I saw what Simon was doing for his community, and I was determined to collaborate with him with hopes that I could also learn and do the same for my community. It's important for me to interact with communities different from my own, so we can all learn from each other's cultures and share what we have been doing to be resilient. As a person from South Seattle, I'm always looking for ways to give back to the community. To be able to share my talents and teach and inspire is what I live for. I want to thank One Vibe Africa and Simon for giving me the opportunity to witness an incredible program and help take One Vibe Africa to the next level. One of my highlights was to meet one of Kenya's most prominent bands: Sauti Sol, and capture their Seattle tour, which benefited One Vibe Africa.

CARLOS CRUZ

SEATTLE BASED PHOTOGRAPHER

In 2017 my wife told me about Simon Okelo and introduced me to One Vibe Africa. Simon's vision and passion for One Vibe inspired me to volunteer to document the Madaraka Festival held at The Museum of Pop Culture at Seattle Center. I witnessed the hard work musicians, organizers, volunteers, and Simon dedicated to make Madaraka Festival a unique experience. It was humbling to see people from several countries work together despite our differences. I captured the commitment of beautiful people from these cultures, coming together for such a great cause. I hope that through my photos, you can experience the journey of love and empowerment that starts from the Madaraka Festival and affects people globally.

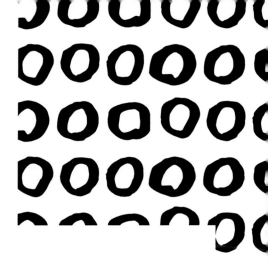

JAY TAYLOR

SEATTLE BASED PHOTOGRAPHER PNW BASED / MULTI MEDIA CURATOR

I first became familiar with the Madaraka Festival in 2015. I discovered that my friend and female hip hop artist Aisha Fukushima would be performing there with a host of other great musicians. This, coupled with my interest in concert photography, caused me to reach out to the festival staff in hopes of covering the event. After being invited to participate as a volunteer and meeting the Founder Simon Okelo, I began to learn about the mission and goals of One Vibe Africa. Their goal of inspiring, educating, and empowering the development of the creative potential of young people in Kenya is one that I support.

The Swahili meaning of the word Madaraka stands for freedom. The efforts of One Vibe are integral to that freedom for African youth and the future of Africa. As an African-American, this is important to me because I believe that the strength of African-Americans as a people is interconnected with the strength of the motherland. By donating my photography services to One Vibe, I hope my contribution can help further raise awareness, provide visual documentation and lasting memories of the events as well as help promote Madaraka's fundraising efforts to benefit and inspire African youth.

JONATHAN CUNNINGHAM
SEATTLE ARTS COMMISSIONER & JOURNALIST

I was first introduced to One Vibe Africa as one of the lead staff members at the Museum of Pop Culture responsible for programming Madaraka Festival in 2014. After meeting Simon Okelo, it was quickly evident that the Madaraka Festival would be more than just a music and arts event. Madaraka, as envisioned by One Vibe, was meant to be a Pan-African celebration, unlike anything Seattle had ever seen. After months of planning, community organizing, and hard work, the inaugural Madaraka Festival exceeded everyone's wildest imaginations. Performers from all across the African Diaspora took the stage, the building was sold out beyond capacity, and a deep sense of community was felt throughout the entire venue. That feeling of togetherness and unity created in the first year was authentic and magical.

What One Vibe Africa is creating in the Pacific Northwest is challenging to achieve but very necessary. The divide between Africans and African-Americans in this region is real. One Vibe's work breaks that down and unites people from across the African diaspora as one in a region where it is desperately needed. The fact that the proceeds from One Vibe events go back directly to the music and arts program in Kenya is an added bonus. I've watched talented African-American youth in Seattle use their entrepreneurial skills selling the artwork of talented youth from Kenya. This type of intercontinental cultural exchange doesn't happen anywhere else. One Vibe's work in Seattle and Kenya certainly deserves praise.

KENJU WAWERU
SEATTLE BASED JOURNALIST AND ACTOR

I came in contact with One Vibe Africa during Madaraka Festival. I remember going home and thinking I should get involved as the impact of empowerment through One Vibe Africa was evident. I am now substantially involved in the movement, and the excitement seems to have only just begun. Working under the mentorship of Simon Okelo, I continue to learn more about One Vibe Africa and how I can be part of the conversation that seeks to empower youth in Kenya and throughout the rest of Africa. One Vibe Africa is a global movement that will positively impact the lives of many in Kisumu and Africa in the coming years; the aftermath will be felt across many divides.

Using my platform in performance spaces and digital media, I share new insights and perspectives with the intent of sparking others to tell their own stories too. One Vibe's story is shared with my belief in channeling our energy towards empowering others to be better. One Vibe Africa has created an excitement in Seattle and Kenya that has brought people from different backgrounds together in an effort to empower others. The effects will be felt for generations to come. I am grateful for the opportunity to be involved in a movement whose vision is to empower young Africans to be the best they can be.

MACKINLAY MUTSEMBI

MULTI-INSTRUMENTALIST & FOUNDER OF NAIROBI HORNS PROJECT

I learned about the Madaraka Festival in 2015 when I went to play at a smaller festival organized by One Vibe Africa known as Made In Kisumu. Owuor Arunga, who was Macklemore's trumpeter, was the Music Director of the band backing Yirim Seck, Nazizi, Blitz The Ambassador, and a host of other artists there. I also met Simon, Harold, Violet, and other One Vibe team members. I greatly admired the project, its objectives, and its strong community approach. I started speaking to Simon and slowly got involved as a volunteer consultant on organizational development and programming, having worked in the sector previously.

Madaraka Festival and One Vibe have a special thing: A closely-knit people with a strong sense of community, all working together to achieve something special despite the distance and geography that separates them. There is also a powerful sense of ownership amongst the stakeholders to the ideals and programs of One Vibe. Also, having had the good fortune to interact with some of the beneficiaries, and hear their stories and also see how their lives have been impacted by the activities and programs is a true motivation to see how such an organic initiative has morphed into a life-changing and impact-driven organization.

MEG STACKER

NEW YORK BASED PHOTOGRAPHER

In 2014, I worked with One Vibe to coordinate the photography team for the Madaraka Festival in Seattle, Washington. This is how I met Simon and became familiar with One Vibe Africa. My first trip to Kenya was in 2012, where I brought my disposable camera project to an orphanage in the Rift Valley to share photography with the youth and see their world through their eyes. The vision and artistic development that happened with the students incredibly inspired me, and I was eager for another opportunity to return to Kenya. One Vibe was the perfect partner, with their passion, mission, and powerful community.

I flew to Kisumu, Kenya, in 2015 with Simon, a team of innovators and directors from Seattle, and musicians from around Africa and the diaspora. Armed with six Canon digital cameras and gear to give the students, I was beyond excited to mentor the youth, shoot alongside them, see the world through their eyes and learn as much from these gifted youth as they did from me. Using their growing photography skills, we explored perspective, cultural heritage, community, and storytelling. Our week of non-stop adventure included meeting Simon's loving, strong family and witnessing first-hand the impact of their generous efforts for the people in their community. Following the trip, we had the amazing opportunity to exhibit the students and my collective images at Seattle Art Museum. The adventures were life-changing, and I am forever grateful to be a part of the One Vibe Village.

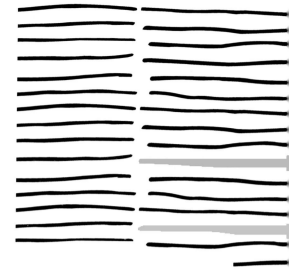

MEKLIT HADERO

SINGER, COMPOSER, MUSICIAN, CULTURAL ACTIVIST

I learned about the work of One Vibe Africa back in 2011 through Founder Simon Okelo. I was excited about the work that the organization was doing around youth empowerment, skill-building, and community organizing on the continent. As an Ethiopian-American woman, I understand the importance of giving youth the necessary tools to build a future that is self-directed and meaningful for them.

In 2012, I had the opportunity to visit Kisumu and see the programs in action firsthand. I was able to meet the youth involved and experience the difference One Vibe was making in their lives. In the years since then, I have watched the organization grow. I had the great pleasure of performing at the 2017 Madaraka Festival at The Museum of POP Culture in Seattle. The event was one of the truest Pan-African experiences I have ever had, and the audience participated with a heartfelt commitment that was inspiring. I'm excited to see One Vibe continue in their efforts, and I wish them all the best in the future.

OTIENO TERRY

SEATTLE BASED SINGER, SONGWRITER, AND PRODUCER

"I don't think I'll ever forget the day I first learned about Madaraka Festival and One Vibe Africa in early 2014. Owuor Arunga invited me to a studio session at London Bridge to do some writing for a song called "Pamoja," which would later be premiered at the very first Madaraka Festival celebration held at The Museum of POP Culture. That was also where I met Simon Okelo for the first time. The energy that everyone brought to that room was so inspirational, and the drive and commitment to helping youth in need were like none I'd ever experienced. Since then, I have performed at every Madaraka Festival, and have been in full support of One Vibe Africa's amazing work, in Kisumu and beyond."

ACKNOWLEDGEMENTS

When I think about the events and activities we've managed through One Vibe Africa since 2008, I also think of the many people that have supported us along the way — knowing that without their support, we could not have been where we are today. This thought humbles me, and when I have the chance to reflect on our journey, I am reminded about the value of having an active community of allies, collaborators, and sponsors.

I may not be able to find and list the name of each person that helped us grow since 2008 when we changed One Vibe Entertainment, a deejay company, to One Vibe Africa, the non-profit organization serving communities in Seattle, WA, and Kisumu, Kenya. Our events in Seattle and Kisumu, alongside our online presence, has created a bridge between Africa and the diaspora. I am truly grateful when I think about the following individuals that have supported One Vibe in many different ways:

Thanks to my mother, Seline A. Akinyi, who since 2008 has allowed One Vibe Africa to use the entire space at Young Generation Centre without paying rent to implement our activities in Kenya. Brie Stranahan has been our biggest individual donor, and I am grateful for the trust that she has had in One Vibe and in me since 2009. Jon Conte and Meg Kerrigan, my in-laws, have been consistent with their support. Rebecca Okelo, my wife, has taught me a lot. While she has been one of the biggest and most loyal supporters of my work with One Vibe, she has also been one of the few people who have given me consistent constructive criticism. My siblings, Violet Achieng, Steve Okoth, Herald Otieno, and Lavender Toya, have been deeply involved and sacrificed a lot of opportunities to see to it that we continue growing One Vibe. I am grateful.

There are close friends and other allies involved as board members in Kenya and Seattle. Tim Thomas, Wael Abou-Zaki, Yirim Seck, Abigail Lynam, Njuguna Wagishuru, Dana Roth, Dee Endelman, Zach Anderson, and Owuor Arunga. I am grateful for all the hours we spent together in Seattle, working towards this vision that is continuously growing. Robert Karanja, Abdulqadir M. Omar, Isaac Oloo, Violet Achieng, Duncan Odhiambo, Maurice Omusolo, Victor Odhiambo have spent years strengthening our foundation by serving as our board of directors in Kenya, and I am very grateful. We have also had friends that have always stood with us as advisors and people that we have looked up to for inspiration such as Boniface Mwangi, Nikkita Oliver, Jonathan Cunningham, Priya Frank, Geoff Fitch, Leah Awino, Marie Kidhe, Vivian Philips, Ebony Arunga, Marcia Arunga, LueRachelle Brim-Atkins, James Miles, Tilo Ponder,

Willy Oppenheim, Rhonda Lee, Margaret Larson, Larry Snyder, Austin Yuen, and Solomon Dubie.

The artists that have performed at our events are key to the impact we have had. They have helped us reach larger audiences through their network while we also have an opportunity to introduce our community to their work. Thank you to the following artists and musicians who have given time and offered services to us in ways that have helped us grow: Sauti Sol, Blitz The Ambassador, Jusmoni, Dax Lion, Zack Okello, Babaluku, Ja Waan Larue, Yirim Seck, Naomi Wachira, Caleb Cunningham & PLH, Naomi Wamboe, Tamao George Yasutake, Yaddi Bojia, Meklit Hadero, Gabriel Teodros, Otieno Terry, Singer Dynamq, Teo Shantz, Aaron Walker-Loud, Aisha Fukushima, Owuor Arunga, Black Stax, Daniel Pak, Kamau Ngigi, Mazigazi Band, Karun, Pyramid Band, Big World Breaks, Choklate, Nik West, D'Bi Young Anitafrika, Fama Ndiaye, Chris Brummel, Jaisen Buccellato, Chris Poage, Bill Jones, Nelson Bell, Thione Diop, Allexion Thomas, James Nathaniel Reed, Aramide, Atuanya Priester, Art Borders, Khaligraph Jones, Ben Soul, Nafsi Huru, Mazzi & Soul Purpose, Musa Jakadala, Kriss Darlin, and Kouyate Arts.

Finally, I want to deeply appreciate the photographers who contributed to this project, especially Meg Stacker, who has stood with us since we started working in Seattle and has traveled to Kenya with us to initiate the Piga Picha Project aiming to place cameras in the hands of youth instead of guns. I also appreciate Carlos Cruz, Tristan Seniuk, Kariba Jack, Truong Nguyen, Jay Taylor, Mujale Chisebuka, Suzy Bichl, Rayna Miller, and other photographers that I may not have included. I also want to sincerely thank Kelly Powers and Dana Roth for spending hours editing the text for this book.

Thank you to Angelique Davis and Christopher Conte for generously and diligently working with me as mentors and official copy editors on this book.

I am so grateful to all of the members of the One Vibe community in Kenya and Seattle and those who took their time to write short stories and testimonials about One Vibe Africa.

Asante Sana,
Simon Okelo,
Founder & Executive Director
One Vibe Africa

Rocky Dawuni
Grammy Nominated Ghanian Artist

As an African musician who has dedicated to the importance of art and music in social development, I was extremely inspired by this effort and understood the long lasting impact this important work contributed to the empowerment of the local environment.

Meklit Hadero
Singer, Composer, Musician, Cultural Activist

"As an Ethiopian-American woman, I understand the importance of giving youth the necessary tools to build a future that is self-directed and meaninful for them."

Rayna Miller
Colorado based Photographer

"As an artist myself, I was able to find my own creative identity through One Vibe Africa's large network of artists and musicians."